Praise for *archipelago*

"In Laila Malik's *archipelago*, we face the future like we face the sea or the desert: any great expanse we try to love, cross, or become. Malik's vocabulary is a bridge—littered with secrets, inside jokes, careful references—that carries us over various landscapes, oceans, the wreckages of capitalism, colonialism, and climate collapse. A play on words is a play on politics because 'history is a weapon of mass destruction.' Encyclopedic in its cataloguing of our failures, spellbinding in its refusal to give up or into hope, this debut collection is a map of our devastations and desperation in equal parts. From the first poem 'all your grandmothers have stopped cooking' to the epilogue 'irreconciliation,' Malik deftly engages with the contemporary imaginary to unravel 'treacherously translucent memory' in the 'nation of unanswerable questions.' 'Forever incanting' across tense, like waves, this collection defies the sweeping tide of tragedy to attend to the molecular, the grains of rice, life, sand, and story alike. Evolutionary and environmental, reverent and reverberating, with rhythm and with rhyme, Malik's words bounce across the page and back into our ears and mouths. From 'oceans of indifference' to 'coastlines [which] eat their feelings,' *archipelago* stretches across the dirt-sure truth that 'embracing sand / becoming prayer' is the key to turning 'all this breaking / into something beautiful.'"

—SANNA WANI, author of *My Grief, the Sun*

"This is a carefully chosen title—what is an archipelago, if not the geographical expression of multiplicity? *archipelago* by Laila Malik is the poetic expression of the geographic, then—a host of voices, overlapping, harmonious, discordant, dark, and humorous in turns. Grief can make an island of anyone: these poems can bring you to new shores."

—NASSER HUSSAIN, author of *SKY WRI TEI NGS*

"There is so much movement in *archipelago*, but the meditations on home vis-a-vis the Gulf are most exciting for their rarity—this may be the first full-length poetry collection in English to take the Gulf itself as its subject matter. The impulse to erase the place you are in because it is erasing you is too strong. Yet though they dwell on the discomfort, vulnerability, and potential violence of not-belonging, these poems feel equally at home everywhere, moving very naturally and horizontally between parts of Canada, the Arabian Gulf, East Africa, and South Asia, reminding us that migration and movement are written into the very histories of these regions."

—NOOR NAGA, Scotiabank Giller Prize–shortlisted author of *If an Egyptian Cannot Speak English*

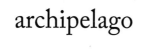
archipelago

archipelago

Laila Malik

Book*hug Press
Toronto 2023

FIRST EDITION

Library and Archives Canada Cataloguing in Publication

Title: Archipelago / Laila Malik.
Names: Malik, Laila, author.
Description: Poems.
Identifiers: Canadiana (print) 2022045809X | Canadiana (ebook) 20220458278
   ISBN 9781771668170 (softcover)
   ISBN 9781771668187 (EPUB)
   ISBN 9781771668194 (PDF)
Classification: LCC PS8626.A4395 A73 2023 | DDC C811/.6—dc23

The production of this book was made possible through the generous assistance of the Canada Council for the Arts and the Ontario Arts Council. Book*hug Press also acknowledges the support of the Government of Canada through the Canada Book Fund and the Government of Ontario through the Ontario Book Publishing Tax Credit and the Ontario Book Fund.

 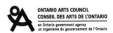

Book*hug Press acknowledges that the land on which we operate is the traditional territory of many nations, including the Mississaugas of the Credit, the Anishnabeg, the Chippewa, the Haudenosaunee, and the Wendat peoples. We recognize the enduring presence of many diverse First Nations, Inuit, and Métis peoples and are grateful for the opportunity to meet, work, and learn on this territory.

for d & a, my lodestars across all the timelines

Archipelago (/ˌɑːrkɪˈpɛləgoʊ/ ARK-ih-PEL-ə-goh), a cluster, collection or chain of islands, or sometimes a sea containing a small number of scattered islands.

I am mere dust. The desert hides itself in me.
Against me the ocean has reclined from the start.

—Agha Shahid Ali, *Call Me Ishmael Tonight*

prologue

all your grandmothers have stopped cooking

this is how we know the world is ending.

the grandmothers have set down
their dois and there is no succession plan.
the grandmothers are stubborn
in their armchair naps, dogged in their deafness.
committed to crosswords and ipads, days punctuated
by scheduled medications and short-lived, rheumy rages
about rain and satellite dish reception.

you will ask me for the family shalgham recipe.
i will nod as though i have waited all my life for this, and
i will launch whatsapp inquiries and google investigations
seeking a legend to the map of your veins.
i will ask whosoever still breathes and cares, whosoever
holds fragments unbloodied with grudge.
i will stitch the patchwork and call it our flesh.

we will not use mustard oil because it is banned
in this country as well as unneighbourly. also because
erucic acid will kill you. we will buy garam masala
from the desi store, some sweaty stranger's measure of
spices grown, ground and packaged in an undisclosed
facility marginally closer to your so-called point of origin,
misting carbon across oceans to get to you. i will cross-
check whether a shalgham is a standard turnip or some
other hyperlocal brassica, and fret over the algebra of red
meat. beef is too tough, lamb too distracting, goat is rangy
and what in god's name is mutton.

                    behind this, planet whispers
                    sit like lead on the guilt gullet.

i will utter silent prayers over heat that spreads a circle
across the glass-top stove and into the steel pot, feeble-
bottomed but stout with on-my-honour promise to protect,
no old-world cancer castaways on my watch.

and bhun. bhun like a grandmother, like your life depends
on it.

> if a shalgham is not bhuned
> and no grandmother is there
> to seize the doi from your
> hand, is it

> still a shalgham?

we will sombrely proclaim this the alchemy of our
dna. we will perfect the dish, imagining
the grandmothers into a kodachrome era with brighter
flavours, better fashion, more precise truths. tongues
warmwagging, dois aloft.

> we will set it on a bed
of basmati, ignoring inner voices that ask which grains
were collected and deposited en route. we will use forks
because we have forgotten how to use fingers, and also
because germs. we will imagine the future secure.

we will chew thoughtfully. we will summon every ounce
of effort to enjoy this resurrection of memory, forgetting
until a grandmother cackles, *"gonglu!"* between
mouthfuls that they had a whole other word for it,

that there never was

> a recipe.

I

precambrian

acacia honey

taproots of the undead
suction secret life from nitreous skies
burrowing a sediment archive

this last ancestor, anticline islanded
garlanded by a filth of lovers with sweet
skins, card vessels stained black with ambrosia
barkbloodied with the passion of
a thousand dull rust blades

                                    —all the while, worker bees
                                    beat veined hamuli across
                                    oceans, heave pollen dreams
                                    swollen with home fictions
                                    off to pull nectar from salt—

remember when they called it *two seas*
drunk on an earth that could birth twins,
sweet & saline, beginning
a life's work of dissolution

just humans airswimming
dry-eyed, clumsylimbing

just humans still fingercounting
camels & petrochemicals

throats slowfilling with wet fire
engulfing true names & membranes
tsunamis & tectonics birthing new horizon lines

just humans still dancing
fidjeri feet on a rising tide

the organic properties of sand

before you were born, gods traded in silences
worked blood into earth, mud wombs hosting
tiny hominid spines, ever fetal-chording serpents & seeds
you, an eastbound bird
brighteyed millennial, aluminum-husked
god your own way from up there, grace
sand with a stopover snickertini
eyerolls behind glass
just dust & towers
tumbleweeding

                                        naked eye babyblind to beyond

teeming life stories of particulate
matter, nevermind pleistocene mollusksongs
still circling

nevermind the first flood
gilgamesh & his jigsaw heart
necropoli of eternal youth
each generation with brave new names
breathless, bloodthirsty with hope

or oil rigs. drill bits spew flecks
of black gold, nevermind hungry
blue eyes, fine aqueous membranes
perforated en route cocktailing
sweet into brackish (so sorry)

                                    nevermind only the poor know
                                                thirst

in the desert
when sun sets on aurum & crude
we still dream water

afterdark confessions, coastlines eat their feelings
fading memory of mangroves buried alive   nevermind
                                                          last rites for dying coral

history is a weapon of mass destruction, you return to babylon

lounging against loot, pain-
stakingly woven by brown hands trading
fables with false idols, *monopoly money,*
disneylands for gluttonous sheikhs

                                                  gulping great drafts
                                                from tiny slivers of god

just kids going home

we are not the first girls to walk the desert alone but we don't know this yet.

hajar and the seven sprints, parched and panicked between two mountains, water for the dying baby, hajar and the millions of others with bones and names and babies long since dissolved into the sand.

                                   we too are thirsty. we are not the first girls.

this endless stretch between school and home is so tiny you could stand on the roof, like ami sometimes does

throw a stone, which she would never

                    if you had a strong arm and if you missed the dhobighat,

jahangir the towering irani security guard for american army school children might look up and wiggle his eyebrows before flashing you his widest smile.

          i am not dragging trails in the sand with my favourite blue canvas shoes
          because it is hometime so you can't fault me

     but those girls alone in the desert before us knew to shroud and mask
                    battoulahs like beaks flashing gold between rocks
                         alert to the light sleep of surrounding teeth
                              knowing well how this kind of lonely

daylight bleaches safety out of shadows.

we are not mothers or babies or daughters of this desert and
we are not children of the american army but here we are in bluejeans
bright tshirts and backpacks

trudging home through molasses heat
sweat pooling the smalls of our backs, each step a labour.

my 16-year-old sister's long black curls
swing free and incongruous
around her shoulders

           as she flashes me hot-embered glares.

    it can't be me this time because it's hometime.
    every step a small freedom from midwestern mr. reust with his math quizzes and
    "i ate your pencil."

but the sun cooks hardest between dhuhr and asr.

humans dead to the day under slowspinning ceiling fans, but out here
                jackals stalk sands for fools
                and outliers like us.

in english we spell desert with one s because it is made of hunger.
in urdu we call it registan because it is its own republic.
in arabic they call it sahra, even though this is an oasis, even though
            ancient waters still stir below.

the boys must be close to my sister's age but to me they are feral, appearing one
  by one on the horizon, gliding in slow silent formation toward us on bicycles.
           sinewy and copper, beautiful and terrifying.

    one day she and i may gallop the midnight shoreline
    with boys something like these
    but for now they have begun the wide circle.

      languorous, hands-free, tossing the occasional word our way
        little shots to kick up dust at our feet, see us dance
      in arabic and broken english. my sister's pace quickens
           and i follow suit

but i am not of interest
with my scrawny eight-year-old body
salt-encrusted strands of hair plastered to my neck.

we are not babies, we are not mothers
not the first girls.

they dip in and lean out,
this sultry, sinister choreography a sawt circle shrinking tighter
around her body as i struggle confused, trying to find her between gaps

in this moving wall of boys on bicycles
hurling their shrapnel mix of words with mounting speed, force, aim. i see flashes

of her red tshirt and black hair, hear her warning snarl, glimpse the whitewhite
teeth of jackals awake and hungry at ungodly hours.

if geometry is the study of isometry groups,
then a centre is a fixed point of all the isometries
that move the object onto itself.
my sister is the centre and the circle is closing

and i am too small too futile to help her.

it is hot, so so hot between dhuhr and asr
and the roads are empty because
all the humans are asleep.

her growl is otherworldly.

her arms muscled, they are tennis arms and volleyball arms
arms she uses to block my flailing assaults for attention with halfsmiles

these arms i hate and wish for.
but there are maybe seven boys on bicycles
and she is only one 16-year-old girl alone because

now i am a meteor orbiting outside the circle and
i don't know what they might do on this empty street
under the scorching concave of this sun
                    but i know i cannot stop it.

                    they are close enough for her to smell musk
                    count each droplet of sweat on upper lips
                    close enough that thighs flex to hold
                    this taut ambit. close enough
                    to reach out a hand

        now a heel grinding dust
                    now two wheels spinning to a halt

                            now five fingers closing tight
                    around the smooth skin of her forearm

                close enough to see the ridges of a thumbnail
                                            now
                                a flash of metal
                            close enough to see
the pattern on her silver cuff is script, close enough
                        to read the ayat
                            and now a shift in the air.

jackal blood cools to boy blood, bicycles brake and skid in the dirt.
eyes fall, terse words volley the air between them as they break formation
                                        turn away

                begin the slow weave back to the village.

            we are all human again
            we are all just kids going home

even if her sweat smells different now, even if

                            we will never speak of it.

cutlery

you could be arab
there is a metal fork suspended between rawan's thumb and forefinger.
a typhoon of adolescents scrape cutlery across stainless-steel trays
clustered by designer label and survival ranking, hooting, mouth-breathing
anxiety into open air.

> rawan's eyes fixed on suneeta
> but her words are arrows
> aimed at me.

you don't look pakistani

> something needs explanation but i am locked in silence.
> child of stone floating
> in a growing moat of sweat.

rawan, drunk on diet pills with freshly straightened hair
butterflying from the soft bread roll of childhood into newly sharpened limbs
testing her vicious, blossoming reach.

rawan's entourage, fume-coifed daughters of bankers and minor royalty
clad in the united colours of benetton
staring with naked admiration at the spectacle unfolding.

> and suneeta.

> deep, dusty mahogany, like the dhows that still line the coast.
> like the shirtless, sun-baked men imported to climb scaffoldings
> move rock without hardhats.
> like nabeel al afdhal's manservant
> standing impassive at the next table where nabeel bellows

jaldi! jaldi! tum h'maar hai!

as the englishboys wag their heads and snicker
jaldi, jaldi, birdie num-num
palms clasped in prayer
at the grown man holding a crumpled dairy queen bag.

suneeta, thinner than rawan, a thin that is bones hung loose under paper skin.
the wrong kind of thin, thin that was always thin
the spindly, hungry hindi kind, wrapped in lurid, ill-fitting synthetics
that smell like formaldehyde and curry leaf.

the kind they call *housemaid*, trudging along dusty roadsides
clutching futile black umbrellas under a beating sun.
decades before rawan herself takes arab girlfriends on a yogic spacation to goa.

i don't know why suneeta is at this table.
i don't know why i am at this table.
i only wanted to eat, but this is not turning out to be an eating kind of lunch.

even your name is arabic

my mouth a mud puddle.

i cannot tell her this is a mistake, i'm not meant to be here.
my name, a thing that stretches into a dark universe beyond arabic.

my name, a betrayal. the fork rocks recklessly

between her fingers.

and then

suneeta
my fork fell again.
get me another.

all the girls entranced, staring at the fork still hanging from rawan's fingers.
eyes locked, suneeta stands slowly.

don't forget
            rawan says
                        don't forget
                        to take the dirty one back.

                  the fork bounces twice

as it hits the floor and for the fifth time this lunch hour
                        suneeta bends
                              picks it up and begins to
walk to the cafeteria kitchen.

miskeena one of the girls breathes and
                      rawan's head jerks like a falcon.

you feel bad? you like her? why, lamees,
you want to french her?
                      ew, disgusting, rawan, haraam alayk!

rawan's mouth a thin line plays with something like a smile.

suneeta!

suneeta stops but does not turn.

don't take too long in there
with your boyfriend, amitabh bachchan

        jaldi,
            jaldi!

                      the girls erupt
                desperate laughter, gasping fish
                      dying for air.

there is a fork at the side of my tray.
sweat on my neck cooling. suneeta has disappeared into the kitchen, where

serving staff who look like her are waiting.

she doesn't have to say a word.

charred grain

madam keens a warning siren;
the basmati is burnt.

soft bodycreamed & carated,
eyes pool, bangles wring, she
curses between broken breaths

> *the maid despoils the future*
> *children unspool the past*
> *siblings poison the present*
> *her own self stretches sorry*
> *across every tense.*

madam's flesh only cools caressed by glass
encased butterskin
meatlocker mercedes, oceans
from her heatsick childself
scuffing shoes up the seventh redsoil hill
lungs full of rich german tire dust
pocketfisting sweat around
a shattered spectacle lens

soothed now by this grassgrafted dominion of sand
caringly cairned with soviet bonechina saltwater pearls french chiffon wrapped
in the smoke of burnt basmati.

they say, *it broke my heart*
like a heart could snap clean & instant

hearts break so slow you never see it coming
bones crack across years of gentle traction

great continents breathing deep
tectonic sighs for all the extinct words.

in the kitchen the riceburning maid flexes,
relaxes brown forearms scrubbing charred
grain from titanium

sings hymns in low monotone she'll build
a concrete home for her own farflung
blood, even god's worst flood

cannot wash away.

grain II

the womb that hosted you is not the beginning.

before her, there were her own mother's fingers, sifting kernels in a shallow tin pan.

you have your mother's hands

before that there were too many children and not enough rooms, an endless expanse of outside, a father in the dark with the warm circle of an oil lantern, and a leopard's yellow eyes watching from beyond the circumference.

there were wealthier cousins, more worldly more sophisticated, on our side only one type of houseboat beauty and brains grimly tilled against a shimmering sea of arched brows and upturned noses. there was a wary standoff, a triangle of mutual surveillance with barely concealed teeth.

diaspora, a fetid, unfurling language.

before that.

before that there was a stroke.

there was her mother squatting on a low stool before a chulla, flipping rotis like a factory worker in a time and place where there were not yet factories, only mothers who mass-produced endless streams of children. there was a pickup truck, one pair of shoes per year (bata leather, to last 12 months of red dirt).

before that there was a newly betrothed 14-year-old, carefully adding numbers longhand in her ~~father's~~ husband's accounts book.

before that there were stories that had to be extracted with forceps without general anesthesia, stories birthed in bloodclots, stories we clad with iron until they were safely reabsorbed into our flesh, vanishing twins to fold us back into earth.

before that we ate some other unspeakable grain.

2

petroleum by-products

the first gulf war

you will think i am writing to you.
i must be; who else is there?

i am caught in your stare
in the airless stairwell before school broke

on an island boiling over.

a well-kept breath,
scorpion trapped in amber.
i am 16;
soon you will drop unseen from school into something stranger.

the last time i was home
(your home, i have no home,
even a sandbar is better than nothing,
beware the person without a country—
she has no country to lose)

i stood on the oil slick east coast, faced
iran at twilight, turning my back
from the sea only long enough
to script this message in the sand:

>   *somewhere else*
>   *something is happening*

for all my wintering since,
the long dry spell has parched me for poison.
no one has loved me
quite like you didn't.

we ignored the 5,000-year-old temple ruins

that lived behind us.

you spent all your father's rage
drank his spirit, stole his car
bleary with purpose listed wildside ways
soundtrack blaring velvet underground crossing
the desert between us

silentstagger slow motion break&enter
sulfurgrain jasmine family
garden you handpicked my own
little dirty rocks sculpted careful cairns
pocketed forgettable relics to slip me
wordless tomorrow at school
whitesun bleaching your blackringed eyes

"mama لحظة
خمس دقائق*"*

we were mudbound before the war
brought skyeyes skyears skymouths
luridplastic telephone hearth of every home
you and i crouched awkward in alcoves breath held
pulsepromise of every rotary spin
sheltered from circling parents
lip to ear whispering spirals across
buried fibre optics

i have to go
my refrain

the only thing you have *to do*
is die

your voice always sliced
softest

                    but i didn't want to die yet

did you know the temple was three-in-one?
sediment stacked like the multiverse, orbited fivetimes daily
gossamer calls, muedhins on everywind
greater & lesser gods walked a fine tessera of straight paths

but you don't get to be right
because you outlive friends

                              & enemies

2 years before you stopped calling
25 before the obituary
5,000 now and everywhere on the map i still maybe
see you in shadows because

kafala

there was no road here.

the desert was the liveliest
of dead things, ask
all the secret snakes
& scorpions ask
the sky & sand how they loved so hard
the whole horizon melted into memory.

i really oughtn't be
gliding moonlessly
through mist on this plastercast asphalt
deathgripping a steering wheel
tensing my metatarsal above the gaspedal

nightpierced by the long jinnwail
cetacean mercedes hulking up the sidemirror
straight for my meridian.

she could be a woman windmilling
her own careening wheel while
babies tumbledry in the backseat
face like a warning flare.

she needs me

         to
         stop.

breechbirthed by the car door
i back into this strange fate a newborn dazed

under ochre highway haze
bare before a black abaya that swells like a sail with dark winds.

transfixed, i do not recite the kalimat
            i do not check the direction of her feet

        you throw bottle you break glass where you from who your sponsor

stabs a weaponfinger at tempered glass dividing her &
her babies, prismed with a fine fracture flowering fractal into the future.

i didn't throw anything   i don't like bottles.
i write news columns   on garbage i eat
local.   i don't always shave
        my legs. the ladies
gape.

                            who your sponsor
                                your sponsor

i don't have a sponsor.

i have one
mother
one
father
two
sisters.

i have skin that bakes quickly
hair that coils midnight escapes

lying amber eyes & a tongue that curls
around every wrong alphabet.

i have a memory of friends
faded far beyond oceans.

i have what they call a boss.
an englishman built of straw & bloodshot eyes

broken capillaries & beerbreath, hired to strip me
of a million years of schooling in exchange for

      a faceful of spit
      a fistful of fils.

i have a blue passport. but
                  your accent still chokes me.

i'm coming from the one
and only time i will ever go to a sheesha café with
daughters of the pakistani ladies' circle.

      i was trying to go home.

one hour late, my parents do something like sleep waiting
for police to puncture their prayers

your sponsor, who your sponsor

maybe woman with bedlam babies
my sponsor might be your husband

licking yellow teeth
across the sheesha café he will

rage when he sees the fractal crack flowering
across his driveway.

i didn't throw any bottle
maybe it was a stone

kicked up from tires scratching rescue notes on this nonroad

                    maybe mine
                                        maybe yours

ask the sky woman of fissured glass maybe

i am your
        sponsor.

vanishing axes

maghreb solitude. slowrise symphony of muedhins
each call its own constellation circling
up minaret to fresh, dark heavens.

whitewashed concrete fades in fallen light
truths speak sideways through

failing shrub geometries
ironbarred windows
peeling green shingles housing
colonies of desert rats.

chinese mangrove weep
sweet leaves on neighbourscrub. eyes cut
over lines crossed. hearts parched
with pistolsilenced love.

we built lifestories on leased sand
there was no other earth. archipelago rose
just to watch the sun
                         set over the gulf.

we pounced seized drilled
breached carved spilled
drank all the fish in the sea

                    magicked water into waste.

our mothers & daughters ripped ligaments across obverse axes
horizons flatlined into an armspan of forever.

here, we strange few insisted
ending our stories with unspelled tongues

embracing sand
becoming prayer.

majnun

to whom it may concern:
she did not die in the desert.

notwithstanding the crushing honeyweight of
all your songs & stories, urgent ululations

heaving oceans of upturned
hands. yes, dark rhizomes unfurled

burning bellies tucked behind schooldesks. yes
her body swayed molten, blackeyed rapture.

something about tribes, sure yes, he roamed possessed
starved for her skin, scent or

some other bloodsucking seduction. yes, no
you kept her safe,

locked inside bad metaphors, sealed sacred
with untouchable folktruths.

she lied.   she lied so well
each lie a lick

of poison laced with love, until
she was the poison itself.

14 types
of ancient lie & they all galloped wild

mares tracing moonlit lines
where sand tongues water

only stopping to hold her name
up to starlight

lovingly wash each soiled facet
                    all that holy use.

he was her brother. flesh its own truth &
yes, her howl splintered heaven.

but she learned to stop swallowing.

no.
she is not waiting for the future

to unbraid her hair before bed
fingers to trace wishes on her skin

warn him now if he approaches
                    closed lips hide cuspids.

she licked the poison
until she was love itself.

sing ghazals into the desert but no
                    she did not die there.

if you ask her, beloved
she will say she is still

                    not sorry.

3
half-life of exile

rites

the flesh under my hands no longer you.

i keep my touch light. your limbs dense with silence. my clumsy fingers
remember.

we wash the body you wore. palms flood water through this new landscape.
here a hollow. an old oasis. illusions.

i'm sorry i love you ya illahi help us take her gently i know you're gone i love you

each mouths her own prayer.

there will be an unstitched white shroud. we turn your head east gently press
each eye shut to allow birth. then earth

in spades and fistfuls. gift of a billion bacteria to greet you.

another life begins without map.

wrong bones

this one is not a friend.

it is not distance or length that makes it unbreachable, not skull-crushing depths. not the songs of souls riding the last right whales beyond the horizon into never again.

there are mystical ecosystems of prehistoric micro-organisms, tucked away within subaquatic thermal vents. it is the planet's tallest mountain range, hiding in plain sight. seabed a powder of crushed human bones. they are the wrong bones.

not a friend. not even an enemy. only a great, churning ocean of indifference.

there was once a strong swimmer, who was you. you swam mostly at night, but never in open water. that was strictly forbidden, and also a bit frightening; you were a deeply committed coward. you swam circles in a small rectangle of flaking paint. you were a wrong whale in saltsuctioned water, swimming circles in a rectangle. but you swam. in warm water, under a black ocean sky.

this time the marrow knows, when you sink ankle-deep into a black new brunswick shoreline scanning the horizon for any trace of home, you have arrived squarely

in the wrong place at the wrong time because

here you are facing the same direction as always, simpering at the slightest mention of foam combing clotted grit.

unmoored you don a kufi, or ink kufic script into the
skin on the back of your neck

       where you can't see it

to remind you how real feels.

these are not verses you knew. you crossed this ocean.

zero bridge

they told you lotus flowers were big where you came from.

they were cooked in a curry-like stew. who knows if it was really curried, where would curry leaves come from so far north? anyway the spices of your origin story were strange and woodsy to you, generations away, on an island in a still gulf simmering between two great rages.

lotus flowers sprouted from the lake in the centre of the city. fresh-faced little girls and young men wore them behind their ears, and visitors swooned and serenaded under the ice-capped mountains with the sheer romance of it all.

but mountains scare you.
the ocean is violent, but at least it moves.

there were seven ancient bridges in the city, arched over a river that tried for reconciliation. they measured time backwards, numbering the bridges as they wound upstream. one day, they built an eighth bridge downstream of all the others. they solved the space-time conundrum by naming it *zero*.

or possibly the contractor was deaf.

the last time you visited, there was no sewage system. everyone's shit souped in the lotus lake. people simply threw garbage out their windows and watched it pile into steaming mounds that rose by the day. mini-mountains in the mountains. no little girls or young men wore flowers behind their ears. no soldiers wore flowers behind their ears.

the last time you visited was a breath between bombs.

they said where you came from was the most beautiful place in the world. it was cold. everyone sat on the floor all the time. the floor was warmed by embers burning eternal from below. the women hugged violently, as though any separation might be final, every reunion a miracle. as though they secretly hoped to squeeze every drop of life from one another. sometimes the embers blossomed into a fire that swallowed the dry tinder of all that longing in its own loving embrace.

they fed you intestines

> with rice, four people to a plate.
> you never ate lotus, not willingly, not wittingly.

zero bridge was dismantled and remantled, your blood lost interest

> in roots and lotus flowers.

dwindling to a trickle, your blood swayed against 99 names in a darkened room. under siege, your blood tried not to betray itself in english, as it betrayed itself in other languages. your blood sang karaoke under its breath.

> your blood thinned to a treacherously translucent memory.

there are those who conjure places they have never seen. there are those who never leave their city, their locale, their tight triangulations of travel, who stream endless tales of the wonders and vagaries of the world, as though their own blood had spilled for it, as though their very hearts had split and knitted, over and again, until each inch was criss-crossed with scars from other people's stories.

> there are those

who speak of what they know not and tell it better than you with your quick-bitten tongue.

fajr is the loneliest number

no guarantee dawn will actually come, just you peeling your unready self from the dermal womb of darkness, let blood seep to surface. shock sleeping skin with ice water. this is what they call faith. if you were a farmer it might be different, pulled forward by the needs of eager seeds germinating in beds of damp black earth. if your nights were less clinical, unencumbered by phantom squares of busybody blue light. if there were a curfew on keyboards.

i had a friend in the noughts who swung nightly from firewater to fajr.
in primates they call this brachiation. in dubai they called this life.

"you can't even hear the adhan anymore," he marvelled, pupils pinpointing into forever.

or maybe woman is the loneliest number. the best would be for you to pray within the four walls called home, but if you insist on leaving the house like a man, find two sets of interlocking shoulders to pin you into place. this is called love, and there is more love for those who loudly complain about haraam ears poking stubbornly from behind your dupatta. dupatta. resist the word hijab because that will close another set of doors to the histories. to who you were, and all the yous who might still be. hijab will open a door to smoke and mirrors, cloak and daggers, snake and ladders.

better to pray within four walls and call it home, remain safely unseen and unheard, but if you must recite try not to speak, even the walls have ears and your voice is a fitnah that could start wars. mouthing the words is ok but try not to understand them too well, knowledge is for the scholars, who do you think you are.

maybe you should have been a farmer.

maybe there's still time to learn.

or maybe the loneliest is the best of numbers. fajr, the antigravity chamber, the moment when it is impossible to situate the beginning from the end, the top from the bottom. you can try to face something called east but there's no sun yet to guide you and anyway what is east, out there in the multiverse? fajr will free you of shoulders and walls, scholars and wars.

there is no east, there may never be a sun.

hidden lines

when her liver spoke in tongues
the muscles of my mouth slackened
muted by the deafening spectacle of the body at large

my pen paled into paper

when her viscera took centre stage
turning flips, performing convulsion
my breath collapsed into a flatline of awe

                                        i hung up my pen to dry

there seemed no point, finally
to words, dry husks flitting uselessly
tempest of organs
no fitting response but white-lipped belt-tightening

                                                    still
                                                she wrote

frozen in the hubris of good health
my fingers splayed empty
as she gripped her pen within quietly folding limbs

in the family footage i brought laughs not courage but
there come times when the humours

are distinctly unfunny

finally death (shorthand
for something infinitely livelier
an ongoing work in progress
some hidden lines)

sinister miracle
unremarkably pedestrian

                                        spoke more perfectly

letter to my stardust sister

remember the time r. ripped off her silk blouse in the olive garden bathroom
flipped her back to the mirrors
thrust forward the flat map of her chest
eyes wide with something like rage
scars ribboning in all directions

> *this is what it looks like.*
> *ok?*
> *look at me.*
> *i beat it.*
> *this is how it is.*

we nodded, a bit agape
laughed later

remember a time before that you and i lounged
on the reem garden couch sharing clandestine
theories of death? we were almost kids
oblivious to sheathed vagaries of bodies

i took an oath to the soul but you
released yourself to stardust

> *i'm not afraid of dying*
> you told your friends
> *but i worry for them*

we the family
sipped tea into polite oblivion

busy, too busied by
fluorescent flashes of blade
black lines of blood beads
words like *subcutaneous*
sharp needles with shocking
requests of your skin

                                            sounds like retching
                                            sounds like weeping

r., intermittent spectre, head to toe in white
only ten years your senior, looked me dead
in the eye across her notary desk

                                            you are protected

so generous. samosas, smiles, comfort
letters at all the right moments
she even got you in with her own oncologist
balm to our broken
parents

                                      so helpful at your funeral

                                   (though one guest shuddered,
                                       she reminds me of a snake)

switched to all black before prison
(remember how she called our parents
amijaan, abujaan
even stole
their names)

magic lady in the headlines
spiriting dollars between dying
& desperate

sombrely told the court

                              there is no right way to do wrong

still speaking in
some kind of
forked tongues

anyway enough of snakes
and vultures. how are you?

don't tell anyone
when i look out on clear nights
i'm almost sure
it was you

who won

how to season a turkey

if you must work fowl without a blood sister:

1. weep into the baste.
2. slip clammy butter fingers
under dead skin salt
rivers running grim jawlines.
3. brine with blurry hands and
neural supernovas.
4. gently rub raw edges
where you were once
sibling forged.
5. marinate for ten years.

> while you work, your daughters
> —coilsprung on a too-long weekend—
> will unleash wolf howls under low living room ceilings
> send flares of laughter into a darkening universe
> grip elbows and spin
> nipping jugulars with vicious milkteeth

> all the better to learn
> where blood pumps hardest.

6. recall:
when she was this kind of alive
you howled too.

4
kufic

the widow's inventory

colonel hathi broke the day i sold our bed.

i sold it last, because it was the first thing we bought. i worked in reverse, just like when we held hands and lumbered backwards around the new apartment, foot on foot, when it was just you and me and a plastic-wrapped mattress on freshly varnished hardwood. fine dust of plaster powder on kitchen formica, disturbed only by the ceramic elephant mug you gifted me before everything: colonel hathi with the missing trunk.

before we moved in. before babies and the midnight shift, before the slow rising tide of arguments, who should cook and clean and change the diapers, before breaths caught, before the slow sneak of symptoms, hospitals wedging awkwardly into our fledgling family.

i sold the newest acquisitions first, retracing our steps in search of the pivotal moment when the end began. meaningless things like wooden candlesticks, glass ornaments, velour blankets. misguided gifts, throwaway purchases made to deflect the fates.

                                        no one nests when they're dying.

the ikea standards were next: a black lack table, a billy bookshelf. things i lugged alone up stairs by the time you were already lost in the stars, counting down cigarettes. (if ever i was jealous, it was of the cigarettes, that Other Woman, and it was true you couldn't live without them, you didn't.)

i sold them to strangers and, seeking the pure math of fiscal exchange, refused to know their names or any part of their stories.

it got harder after that.

there was no room in the awkwardly contoured shrunkenness of our new space, just me and the children and the you-shaped hole where nothing else would fit. i imagined you into the transactions. bureau for the college girl. desk for the middle-school boy. sofa for the community garden office. we gave them good homes, our dearly departed furniture.

until there was only one thing left, and it was our bed. our wedding bed, so laughably uncomfortable from the start. (was that it, the straw that broke your back, did the end begin at the beginning?) i sold our bed to someone's fresh-faced kid sister, leaving home for the first time to live in the big city. i think she might have been a poet or a painter. she needed a bed, and it was my last hope, so i sold that too.

that night at dinner one of the children was drinking from colonel hathi and what kind of mother gives a child a cup without a handle.

are you sad, mama, are you sad. are you sad your broken elephant cup broke into so so many pieces.

and we continued with dinner at our new ikea fold-out kitchen table, the one i bought from a pregnant young couple moving out of their downtown basement rental, into a brand-new house in the suburbs.

still the heart

i have a meeting with my unicorn this thursday,
says the baby

mama sweats cold, smiles big

baby dissolves
into a   liquid plasma screen

    paper butterfly   slice of plastic birthday cake

        seaglass

              kitten sticker

                  chance clump of playdough

mamahands forage
frantic under sofas and ripe laundry mounds, behind swaying bookshelves,
overstuffed drawers

are you here, little sweatshop unicorn
send me a sign

can't lose the last gift from the late late father
(funny guy
always punctual, early to dead
      eternal jokes)

mama
did you find it?
not yet but not to worry, i know
where it is
i know   i know
all the things

neighbour slips a secret called honest ed's
mama stumbles out mumbling errands, overshoulder applause

such profound primitivism, pinkie pie
would be proud!

(always careful with words no matter how
mundane the parting of paths
still the heart
chokes on every grotesque
unspoken)

steps into a split-level maze, neon dust thick with oldworld glamour
and every kind of

cast-iron frying pan   carburetor   signed silver screen portrait
frozen turkey

chocolate easter egg   hellokitty

underwear

and

a sudden woman in her path

hello which is better?
peach canvas tote, grey one with pockets

mama backs slowly away
falls into the arms of
a uniform

please i need a unicorn
what kind, deadpans ed.

this never-ending darkness
pebbled slush
relentless dust
scuffed boots kick salt and sidewalk
sallow skin under sighing grey corduroys

pupils dart, winter starlings
on a powerline new skin tributaries spring
fresh to grim lipline and an animal howl
escapes, slices clean through
bone lonesome street
cracked white knuckles gripping babybird shoulderblades

YOU CANNOT PLAY ALONE ON THE SIDEWALK
DO YOU HEAR ME

LOOK ME IN THE EYE
AND SAY IT

I WILL NEVER PLAY ALONE ON THE SIDEWALK

in this house we do not play with death

only

unicorns

baby shark

mangrove takes the orphans
mama did her best but

some guy bit her raw
she knew she would bloodfrenzy at the merest

flotsam

    never mind kith
    never mind kin

she sections a cracked heart
into sacs & yolks:

                                                       all i can give you is a headstart

ocean splits, babies bolt
claret comets streak the first salt sunrise for

safety

    root jungle too thick
    for hungry lumbering mothers

eyes shut white against the sting
seven-spined smiles of shank teeth
checks her watch, marks the spot

                                          one day mangrove will feed mama too

urdu

i still moth you
flit above and behind nuqtas, skimming
calligraphic surface despite
genteel curses of aunties and in-laws

wolfstares from cousins
always scenting something unspoken
on our blood

a naani's parchment hands
trembling sheafs of curling script
single bulb warming a birth circle
in fertile darkness between ishaa and fajr

gently pickle the mouth
silverleaf rapids gummed with prim syntax

bow, flow for zealots and
apostates alike

with offerings for the children:
    phantom limbs, feeble romance

see me still mothing
when even my mouth knows better

crooked elbows

1: mountain

they say we walked south with softspun
currency of peasant gold, hand-picked
from goatbellies

elemental chemistries of rice & rain
despot & harvest against idyllic frescoes of
colonial chess maps
yielded chasmic kinds of hunger

(but no one
knows no one
says no one
wrote it down).

what i can tell you about the motherland:

> *crag-tongued, even the lesser himalayas*
> *encircled and swallowed*
> *us whole.*

> *we showed up faithful*
> *in pherans and the needle diction*
> *of long-lost brethren etched*
> *a thousand vengeful nicks into*
> *skin gone soft*
> *from too much away.*

> *no familiar words leapt out to salve*
> *this homecoming.*

> *my 14-year-old body could barely breathe*
> *for lack of seawater. we drowned*
> *in a heady saturation of mustard oil*

to the wailing wanwun
wall of swaying biddies
now runes beyond our range and

seated four to a silver platter
steaming basmati crowned with saffron
and delicately seasoned entrails we betrothed
a sister back to the valley.

the other eloped
with her old friend nicotine; i wept
silent salt tucked within
a walnut armoire. cooling blood
with the scent of musty wool and fresh ziba'd tree.

what did we know about brewing
namkeen wars. we cracked
bones stretching backward
across time only to grab at
fistfuls of glacial air.

2: ocean

in 1896, someone dreamt a great locomotive snake
crossing the continent, horn to lip.

they built a ship of promises
coolies in cold steerage; gentlemen port out
starboard home.

16-year-old khwaja shams, his brother camr
sirs sun & moon; our ancestors were not afraid
to birth constellations.

(there were epic journeys of sisters
named after another solar system. but no one
knows no one
says no one
wrote it down.)

brokering may have begun on that ship;
bespoke kashmiris play cloak and dagger with inner skins.

we know for sure the undulating ocean road began
with bombay. we know mombasa was never the end.

what i can tell you about east africa:

bloodsoil everywhere.
avocados the size of small planets.
kiswahili a melody that will unfetter
some lost part of your heart even as
the people stare
with frank disinterest.

the aloe stands, in the farthest reach of mamajii's garden
taller than your eight–year–old head.
you can scratch your name in it and it will still be there in three years
and in three years you

will still not belong.

3: sky

in 1974 there were mixed feelings.

lucre lost
britons backed quietly away
left all shades of brown mostly conquered
completely divided.

your grandparents folded four generations
arose, etched a westward arrow ever farther from the sun.

like you i was born
on native land.

there may have been a blur of twisted white faces
speeding down the 401
loosing screams like pig-oiled bullets
through open windows

pakigohomepakigohomepakigohome

we know for sure that place called
where there are trees in water
on land at other times known as tkaronto
was not their home either.

4: gulf

i can't tell you anything about al khaleej because
we did not breathe 40 years of our lives
into that sea.

no lingering fishscent of my sister's koi dream
no dusty eucalyptus guarding
her old window. the baobab
& neem she smuggled
as seedlings from nairobi & delhi
did not construct root cities
under the shape-shifting sand of my childhood.

i can ask you to *come here* in perfect arabic &
it will not make me a better muslim, will tell you nothing
about ruddy-cheeked englishboys, tomorrow's slicksuited leaders
unleashing a unionjack ribbon of slurs
out the window of our air-conditioned school bus, nothing
about the pakistani street vendor sprinting, sobbing behind us,
eating exhaust for another 100 fil theft

pakigohomepakigohome

there may have been 1,001 cities of glory
built by a sea of faceless brown bodies
fetching tea building roads falling from scaffolding wiping asses rotting in jails
dying in camps
getting raped in servants' quarters

our stories may be buried
in unmarked graves under seven-star restaurants but
we know for sure

we were never there.

5: daughters

your grandmother's instructions, 1986:
never write anything down

someone might read it.

cautionary tales of families
riven by the weaponous words of wayward daughters
paraded naked on paper for all to see.

we protected our women
with an armour of silence & now
i can give you only half a history.
half of half of half of half times forever
zeno's paradox of invisible women
a bloodline concentrated
on irrelevant endpoints.

                    & still the families rived.

if home is where we have neither stolen land nor spilled blood
where the earth runs thick with our dna

                    there is no home.

only shadowpeople like us
forged with memory shards
into an awkward state of namelessness
painfully perched on someone else's burial ground.

there are plants whose scents, when burned,
will draw us like weeping animals around a fire and
sometimes you make up songs that sound like stories
i heard before i had words.

we can ask the wendat, haudenosaunee, anishnabe, seneca
if we can take cuttings of those stories
and share this soil

maybe they will take root
maybe they already have

we know for sure i have always loved you
will love you forever
& possibly
there is something ancestral in my love &
possibly not.

still today we skate foal-legged on fresh ice
& tonight asleep entwined
against outside storms
you will sweat pieces of ancient dreams
into my crooked elbows

as i pray fierce into darkness

> *let my transgressions*
> *crack open enough space*
> *for little hearts to grow*
> *all this breaking*
> *into something beautiful.*

maybe
even
a whole

new
kind of

story.

epilogue

irreconciliation

i knew a woman who woke up every morning and asked herself
                                        which whistle will i blow today

i knew a woman who shushed
        the chorus of devil's advocates in her mind with freshbaked cumin cookies
clucked and soothed, ironrod everclasped
                                        under tattered frontier skirts

cookies a new brand of colonization;
                        her oldcountry people preferred oldschool tea biscuits
                            with a biscuit, you knew who held the firearms.

time moved safely

            in a straight line, toward the

                        inevitability of erasure.

i knew a woman who woke up every morning to a whistle blowing her
we called her devourspora because she ate all the spores of her origins, spat out
the doubts
                    and grew fields upon fields of unanswerable questions

at first she called this family, then community, then
biting a piece off her tongue and looking both ways before crossing the street
                                        she called it nation

she didn't know or she knew,
her soles had grown spikes and with every step she impaled

                                        survivors

she toiled hard not to think

                of any word for this

                but her nation of unanswerable questions called it

                      <collateral>

fields upon fields

in her spare time she grew native herbs on her balcony, desperate for
pollinators and

                            forever incanting

                        i can't be a landthief if i live in the air

                                  can i

can i can i can i can i can i can i can i can i can i can i can i can i can i can i

notes

all your grandmothers have stopped cooking
Doi is an Urdu word for a cooking spoon.
Shalgham is a traditional Kashmiri and/or Persian turnip stew.
Bhun is an Urdu (and Hindi) word that refers to the culinary technique of
    slowly cooking down a dish over high heat, usually while stirring, so the
    liquid evaporates and the flavours intensify.
Gonglu is another Punjabi word for turnips (alongside shalgham).

acacia honey
Fidjeri is a tradition of call-and-response folk music sung by the pearl divers of
    Eastern Arabia, influenced by East African rhythms and associated with
    supernatural, mythical origins.

just kids going home
Hajar is the Arabic name for the wife of the prophet Ibrahim (Abraham) and
    the mother of Ishmael. According to some accounts, Hajar was led to the
    desert and left there with her infant son by her husband. When she ran
    out of water and her son began to cry from thirst, Hajar repeatedly ran
    between two nearby hills, Al-Safa and Al-Marwah, in search of water.
    After her seventh run, a miraculous well sprang from the ground. This is
    called the Zamzam Well and is located a few metres from the Kaaba in
    Mecca.
Derived from Arabic, Ami is an Urdu word for mother.
Dhobighat is a type of open-air laundry commonly found in South Asia.
A battoulah is an ornate face mask, often with a metallic sheen, traditionally
    worn by women in Eastern Arabia. Some historians claim it entered the
    region via the South Asian state of Gujarat in the 18th century.
Dhuhr and Asr are two of the five daily prayers in the Islamic tradition. They
    take place at noon and in the early afternoon, respectively.
Sawt is a traditional form of Eastern Arabian acapella singing by men that
    takes inspiration from classical Arabic poetry.
An ayat is a verse from the Quran.

cutlery

jaldi! jaldi! tum h'maar hai!—jaldi is an Urdu/Hindi word for quickly or hurry, commonly known and used by non-Urdu/Hindi-speaking employers of domestic workers. This sentence is composed in a type of elite regional pidgin that mixes Urdu, Hindi, and Arabic and is often used by persons of authority to command workers. H'maar is an Arabic word for donkey, a common insult in the region.

Birdie num-num is a famous line from a 1968 American comedy film in which actor Peter Sellers wore brownface to play a bumbling Indian visitor to the United States, ignorant of Western ways. The film was considered a cult classic.

Miskeena is an Arabic word in the feminine form, used to mean pitiful.

Amitabh Bachchan is an Indian actor, enormously popular in South Asia as well as the Middle East in the 1980s.

grain II

A chulla is a traditional South Asian stove used for indoor cooking.

we ignored the 5,000-year-old temple ruins

"mama لحظة
"خمس دقائق"

"mama, wait—five minutes"

The muedhin is the person (traditionally a man) who recites the Islamic call to prayer five times a day from the mosque.

kafala

Kafala is a system used to monitor non-citizen workers in the Arabian Gulf region. The system requires non-citizen workers to have a local sponsor who is responsible for their visa and legal status.

The kalimat is one of six religious phrases often recited by South Asian Muslims.

vanishing axes

Maghreb is the fourth of five daily prayers in the Islamic tradition.

majnun

Majnun, "the mad one," sobriquet of a seventh-century Bedouin poet driven
to obsession by his unfulfillable longing for his beloved. Immortalized
for ten centuries by male writers including Abu al Faraj al Isfahani, Ibn
Qutaybah, Niẓāmi Ganjavi, Amir Khusrow, Nur ad-Dīn Abd ar-Rahmān
Jāmī, Maktabi Shirazi, Hatefi, Fuzuli, Eric Clapton, countless Bollywood
screenwriters, and more recently a New York opera, the tale was described
by Lord Byron as "the Romeo and Juliet of the east" and has been used
to explore mystical concepts such as fanaa (annihilation), divānagi (love-
madness), and self-sacrifice. It has historically been narrated from the
perspective of Majnun.

fajr is the loneliest number

Fajr is the first of five daily prayers in the Islamic tradition.
The adhan is the Islamic call to prayer.
Dupatta is an Urdu word for a scarf loosely worn over the head by women in
various South Asian traditions.
Fitnah is an Arabic word for temptation.

the widow's inventory

Colonel Hathi is an elephant character in the 1967 animated Disney film
The Jungle Book. Hathi is an Urdu/Hindi word for elephant.

urdu

A nuqta is a diacritic mark found in Urdu script. It takes the form of one or
more dots placed above or below a character, and often signifies subtle
nuances between consonants.
Ishaa is the final of the five daily prayers in the Islamic tradition.

crooked elbows

A pheran is a traditional Kashmiri cloak.
Wanwun is a tradition of ritual Kashmiri folk song performed by women. It is
monotonal and sung on a fixed beat, with a spoken-word type rhythm.
Ziba is the Muslim method of slaughtering animals for consumption.
Namkeen is an Urdu/Hindi word for something salty.
Al Khaleej is the Arabic name for the Arabian Gulf region.

acknowledgements

My paternal grandfather was known for the riveting letters he wrote from and to Kampala, Bombay, Lahore. My maternal grandmother's bedroom light glowed amber late into the Nairobi night as she read in Urdu and Arabic, silent and alone. My father has always been a gentle, spellbinding storyteller and a prolific writer with a photographic memory for detail. These, perhaps, are the original gifts, delivered in the generative space between DNA and dogma, and ones for which I am eternally grateful.

While I have been a writer since I could hold a pen, it was Chelene Knight's Advanced Poetry Workshop and her generous ongoing mentorship that allowed this collection into existence.

My early kindred spirits Yoon Sook Cha and Nasser Hussain generously lent eyes, time, faith, and inspiration to earlier versions of this manuscript. I am forever indebted.

Shazia Hafiz Ramji went on to perform editorial magic when I believed there was nothing left to be done. Michel Vrana's gorgeous design was everything I didn't know I had imagined, and artist Meera Sethi miraculously brought me into myself in front of her camera. My thanks also go to Stuart Ross for his fine-toothed copyedits.

To have illustrious poets Noor Naga, Sanna Wani, and Nasser Hussain take the time to read the manuscript and share their reflections was a dream. Publishers Hazel and Jay Millar at Book*hug Press have been a joy to work with, and I couldn't have had a better publishing experience.

Audre Lorde famously said, "Poetry is not a luxury." I might never have given myself permission to visit this ancient and hidden place of possibility were it not for my community of loved ones who held me as I parented through all the losses, and who offered us, me and the children, new hope and open-hearted love. You know who you are, and I am awestruck by every one of you every day.

I thank my mother for the fire she bequeathed us. I thank my sisters for holding open the doorways of possibility. There are not enough words to capture the balance of deep, consistent care, thoughtful adventure, and gracious insight my father provided us.

I thank you, m&z, for always holding our gossamer lifeline to the future with humour, generosity, and unanticipated promise.

I thank my daughters for manifesting themselves, bringing all the meaning into joyous focus.

And I thank the lands—the actual archipelago that shaped me, quietly arcane in the mouth of the Tigris and Euphrates rivers, that place where the waters breathe before Hormuz frees them to wild ocean.

And Tkaronto, territory of the Wendat and Petun First Nations, the Seneca, and most recently, the Mississaugas of the Credit River. My prologue and my epilogue, the ancient watershed that brought me back to life.

Creation of this work was funded in part by an Ontario Arts Council grant.

About the Author

Laila Malik is a desisporic settler and writer in Adobigok, traditional land of Indigenous communities that include the Anishinaabe, Seneca, Mohawk Haudenosaunee, and Wendat. Her work has been widely published in magazines and journals, including *Contemporary Verse 2, Canthius, The New Quarterly, Ricepaper, Qwerty, Room, Sukoon, The Bangalore Review*, and *Archetype*. Malik's essays have been longlisted for five different creative non-fiction contests, and she was a fellow at the Banff Centre for Creative Arts in 2021.